Making the Annual Pledge Drive Obsolete:

How Churches Can Get Out of This Business Once and For All

Making the Annual Pledge Drive Obsolete:

How Churches Can Get Out
of This Business Once and For All

Timothy Dombek and Michael Durall

COMMONWEALTH

Timothy Dombek and Michael Durall

Making the Annual Pledge Drive Obsolete:
How Churches Can Get Out of This Business Once and For All

Published by CommonWealth Consulting Group
2108 Washington Avenue
Golden, CO 80401

www.vitalcongregations.com

Copyright © 2014 by Timothy Dombek and Michael Durall

ISBN 978-1-4675-9755-5

Printed in the United States of America

CONTENTS

From Timothy Dombek

To my parents, Wladislaw "Loddy" Joseph Dombek and Olive Lillian Dombek, who by their example alone taught me to be a generous and faithful steward. To my wife, Beth Dombek, and our son, Jonathan, who are daily reminders of God's unconditional and overflowing love.

From Michael Durall

To San Daugherty, who restored my faith.

Nothing you can purchase, buy, own, possess, or collect;
nor any trip you can take, to any part of the world;
nor any sight you will ever see;
is more valuable than the money you give to others in need.
— Rev. Timothy Dombek

Acknowledgements

Bishop Kirk S. Smith and the clergy and lay leaders of the Episcopal Diocese of Arizona, who for over five years now have listened to me talk about stewardship and offered excellent feedback and ideas to improve my workshops.

For many friends and mentors who have helped us along this journey: Michael Bassoff; Jeff Bradley; Barb and Ralph Bramlett and Grace Church, Lake Havasu City, AZ; J. Clif Christopher; the Rev. Andrew Cooley; Dave Denmon; Bishop Frank and Karen Gray; the Rev. Rip Hoffman; Janet Kaiser; Clyde Kunz; Charles Lane; Mary MacGregor; Carol Maher; Deacon Brian Nordwick; the Rev. Julie O'Brien; Bishop Robert O'Neill; Deacon Ian Punnett; Bishop Mary Gray-Reeves of the Diocese of El Camino Real and Bishop Greg Rickle of the Diocese of Olympia; the Rev. Canon CK Robertson, of the Presiding Bishop's Office of The Episcopal Church; the Rev. Barb Schmitz; the Rev. Susan Snook; the Board of The Episcopal Network for Stewardship (TENS), in particular, retired director Tom Gossen and the late Carl Knirk; and Bishop Steve Talmage and the clergy and laity of the Grand Canyon Synod of the Evangelical Lutheran Church in America, Lucille Sterling and the Southwestern District of the United Methodist Church, and the many Episcopal Dioceses and congregations across the church that have invited me to present Stewardship University to their clergy and lay leaders. Thank you all.

A special thanks goes to Randy Boone, copy editor extraordinaire.

INTRODUCTION

This book is based on the premise that giving money away is just plain fun, whether you have a little, or you have a lot. Being a generous person or family is one of life's great privileges and profound joys.

Having fun with your money should be all that's necessary to say about conducting a successful pledge drive, but alas, churches make it considerably more complicated.

This is not just a book about different ways to ask people for money. More importantly, it's a book about how churches can become worthy recipients of members' charitable giving, an endeavor in which to invest. In the pages that follow, we'll consider two simple yet persistently challenging questions. What kind of people is God calling us to become? And what kind of churches do we yearn for, that we are proud to call our home?

We hope you create a church that brings about a more just and humane world; a church that helps families break the cycle of poverty, aids people in overcoming crippling addictions, assists in providing companionship to the lonely, and takes a public stand against intolerant and hateful speech.

The stakes are high, and the church's work is truly life giving. Getting your money out there and putting it to work provides hope to the least and the lost among us. At its best, charitable giving creates the presence of a living God in our midst. Who wouldn't want to take part?

When you write a check to your church, or to another charity that does meaningful work, it should be an immensely pleasurable experience — that life doesn't get much better than this. Because at the end of the day, it's not a matter of the church requiring money. It's the essential need of the human heart to give, to take flight, to breathe new life, to be one with God.

The church is the one institution that is called to help those less fortunate, and is dedicated to the formation of active followers of Christ. As the Lutherans say, "God's work, our hands."

Anyone of any means can become a philanthropist, among the highest callings to which we mortals can aspire. To each in good measure, the hallmark of a life well lived. The church should be in the business of creating philanthropists who occupy the pews on Sunday mornings; with you, gentle reader, in their midst.

Being a generous person is also a deeply religious act. Many people say they feel closer to God when making charitable gifts than at any other time. Charitable giving is an indispensable means to discover what is truly valuable in our lives, and what is superfluous. Surely, God does not call us to be miserly, greedy, or materialistic, all the while indifferent to the plight of others.

In the trenches

This book is also for the multitude of clergy and lay leaders who long for alternatives to the hectoring aspects of annual fundraising; and for the hearty souls who oversee the pledge drive, arguably the worst job the church has to offer.

All too often, churches turn a joyous ministry into a practice that metaphorically flogs beleaguered parishioners to give money for weeks on end, until they are glad when the pledge drive is finally over and dread its coming around again.

We are cautiously optimistic about the future of the church, but mainline Protestantism faces significant challenges. The church has lost millions of adherents since the 1960s, and these losses continue today. Tweaks to established customs may be insufficient to envision a new tomorrow, and we ask readers to keep open minds about the ideas we propose.

Our hope, dream, and prayer is that your church, of whatever size or faith tradition, will join the ranks of the happiest and healthiest congregations; churches that buzz with excitement, purpose, and meaning because they give a larger than average share to mission and outreach beyond their own four walls. These churches have a *raison d'etre,* a well-defined reason for being.

We'll discuss money in many engaging ways throughout this book, but our foremost purpose is to help you and your fellow congregants discover the manifestation of God in your own hearts, and in your congregation's soul.

4

[Handwritten annotations at top of page: "why I ask = person to person phil to do something — I expect to then say yes"]

4

CHAPTER 1

Let's Cut to the Chase

Everyone off the bench and onto the field.
We are not in the business of creating spectators.
— Policy of many newly-formed nondenominational churches

Just about every problem a congregation encounters, including low-level giving, cost-conscious budgets, and difficulty recruiting volunteers, can be traced to low expectations of membership — the albatross around the neck of mainline Protestantism since the 1950s.

Other than scandals of various types, low expectations of membership is the most debilitating aspect of congregational life ever to come down the pike.

Church leaders, clergy and lay alike, tend to believe that asking people to become dedicated members will scare them away. Low levels of commitment often result from church leaders themselves who joined the church under low expectations, and may be unenthusiastic about increasing their own commitment. They are also hesitant to raise expectations on their fellow congregants, often long-time friends and neighbors. In contrast, many nondenominational churches take the opposite approach. In these congregations, regular attendance at Sunday worship, frequent participation in church initiatives, and heightened generosity constitute the meaning of membership. Such high levels of commitment often result from membership orientation classes that are 35-40 weeks in length.

These churches believe their job is to create members who are strong, able, and looking for some adventure in congregational life. Should this not be the goal of all churches? What is to be gained by keeping parishioners uncommitted and halfhearted?

One of the essential elements in making the annual pledge drive obsolete is creating people who believe they all have a stake, a piece of the action, in forming a church that is deserving of their charitable giving.

Encouraging people in the pews to take ownership of the enterprise is very different from asking them for money. St. Paul uses the metaphor of the church being, "The body of Christ," to which all baptized persons belong. This is the ultimate level of commitment, to live as Christ's body in the world until all of us come to the unity of the faith and of the knowledge of the Son of God, to maturity, to the measure of the full stature of Christ. (Ephesians 4:13, 15-16). A culture of inclusiveness alleviates the attitude that congregants are bystanders, and their charitable giving mainly pays the bills.

Claiming the power of the faith

Mainline Protestantism struggles because it too seldom conveys the message that membership should change our lives in some fundamental way. Unfortunately, in many households, the church is viewed as one activity among many on the family calendar, not the source of an inspired way of living.

Theologian Miroslav Volf once asked, "Why are communities of faith increasingly ineffective at their central task?" His answer is, "Churches do not offer a compelling vision of a way of life that is worth living."[1]

This is not a workbook, with fill-in-the-blanks sections, but we'd like to ask readers to pause a moment, to think, ponder, pray, and talk with your loved ones about a way of life that is truly worth living. We'll include some suggestions later in the book. For now, is defining a life of greater meaning and purpose a central theme of congregational life in your church? If not, might you be the one to introduce this idea?

Or, might you think this is none of the church's business? George Barna, a prominent researcher of American religion, notes:

People expect a church to conform to the will, needs, and interests of individual members. Few people view the church as the pivotal player in the drama, with the attendee following a prescribed role for a predetermined purpose.[2]

In a recent sermon, a Methodist minister facetiously suggested that parishioners sit in their garages for an hour each Sunday morning. After a year, he would ask if they had turned into cars. Obviously, they would not. But he said a lot of people come to church for an hour every Sunday, and they don't turn into Christians. What he didn't say was, "Whose fault is that? Yours, or the church's?" So what are a church and its people to do?

A spiritual life doesn't happen by accident, isn't always cheap, and shouldn't be viewed as coming easily. Few things in life that come easily hold much value.

Higher expectations of membership are the basis, foundation, keystone, bedrock, and underpinning of churches that wish to be healthy, engaged players in the world around them. Lacking this, churches will falter.

Yet even mentioning the subject of higher expectations is a subject that is avoided like the so-called "third rail." Touch it, and risk a high voltage shock!

Here's a skillful way to approach the issue in a more engaging context. Churches should not use the phrase, "Expectations of Membership." The word "expectations" is a red-flag word that carries a negative connotation of, "What do I have to do?" The answer to that question, all too often, includes mundane tasks that people aren't particularly interested in.

In contrast, Membership in Good Standing, or Membership With Integrity, are open and welcoming, something people will strive for. Who wants to be a member in poor standing?

Congregations of all faiths should clarify what it means for an adult to be a member in good standing. Our recommendations include:

• Attending Sunday services regularly. Small miracles occur every Sunday, and people need to gather in community each week. Regrettably, many churches do not emphasize this essential element of the religious life. Nationwide, less than 50 percent of church members attend Sunday worship on a regular basis. A walk in the woods or a stroll on the beach, while enjoyable, are inadequate substitutes.

• Participating in one church program each year that deepens your understanding of the faith. Book groups that read religious literature, small group ministries, and Sunday morning classes are excellent examples of how people can learn to live together more faithfully.

• Participating in one mission or outreach initiative each year beyond your own four walls. Whether it's local or in a foreign country, church people should get their hands dirty on a regular basis. Outreach to the community is the fundamental difference between many established churches and those founded more recently. Established churches believe "church" happens primarily in their own building. So-called "missional churches" believe the church's primary work occurs in the community.

• Reaching the 5-10 percent giving level as soon as possible. This is a minimum, not a maximum. Some people, even of modest means, give away as much as 25-30 percent of their incomes.

• Telling others about the faith. If your church is an interesting place, this will be a great joy.

Some readers may believe the church could never ask members for so much, while others will find the above to be a reasonable rung on the active and involved membership ladder. Church leaders should not fall prey to the excuse, "Everyone is so busy nowadays. No one has time for any of this." Vast numbers of Americans now spend anywhere from four to eight hours per day on some type of electronic device. People find time for what is important.

As for reaching the 5-10 percent giving level, this might be sticker shock for some, but tithing isn't as scary as most people make it out to be. People who tithe consistently claim they don't miss the money, don't really give up anything, and lead more enriched lives. Many people who tithe also report they used to be anxious about their personal finances, but once they began tithing, they didn't worry about that anymore. This is a leap of faith. Do yourself a favor and try it.

Regardless of your view of the above criteria, a clearly defined definition of Membership in Good Standing should apply to all parishioners, young and old alike. An annual Sunday worship service during which members reaffirm their commitment to the church is a moving and heartfelt event.

No successful business, nonprofit organization, elementary school, high school, college, university, hospital, professional sports team, ballet, theater group, symphony orchestra, or any other entity functions on the basis of low expectations.

Regardless of the logic of setting standards, attempts to clarify Membership in Good Standing that raise the bar are likely to bring pushback from congregants, especially those most comfortably settled in. The aforementioned others will probably brush the idea aside because they view the church as having no authority whatsoever in these matters. Keep in mind that churchgoers have undergone decades of training to be noncommittal. Old habits die hard.

But there will also be a segment of the congregation that heeds the call for a more consequential religious life. These are the restless souls, and in them lies the future of your congregation. Some parishes have experimented with a "church within a church" format, often called the Great Expectations Church, that calls members to higher standards and greater involvement. Your congregation may be ripe for this type of experiment.

A low-expectation church does its members no favors, and truth be told, robs them of worthy religious lives. We find this unacceptable. The religious life is an active, not a passive life. The next chapter continues this conversation.

CHAPTER 2

Parishioners as Consumers

Coming to church proclaims that we have not been taken in by the
fern-bar quality of life that passes for reality, the gaudy tricks and
pacifiers of this tedious age. Coming to church testifies that we are
dissatisfied with the second-rate and the second-best.
— Baptist minister Peter Gomes

This chapter delves into a deeply entrenched but little discussed aspect of congregational life: about one-third of members give most of the money and do most of the work. The remaining two-thirds get a low cost, sometimes free ride. This long-established ethos is considered the norm, but we're going to take a second look at this inequitable state of affairs.

Let's begin by returning to the results of another survey, which indicated:

> *People seem to believe that spirituality comes from self-enlighten-*
> *ment rather than a commitment to a faith group and perspective.*
> *They believe religion is a commodity to be consumed, not one in*
> *which to invest. The prevailing wisdom is that religion is some-*
> *thing you draw from, not contribute to. Matters of faith are a*
> *take-only, and not a give-and-take proposition.*[1]

The notion that religion is a product to be consumed and not one in which to invest is a serious impediment to the future of any congregation. A consumer attitude implies that the church functions as a type of retail store. Someone else unlocks the doors, turns on the lights, stocks the shelves, and everything the church offers comes with bargain-basement prices. This type of church is wildly incompatible with a community of faith on a shared journey, with everyone pitching in as they are able.

Inequitable giving

Some readers may believe that two-thirds of the congregation give less because they are poor, have fallen on hard times, or just don't have the money. To this list we would add various levels of household debt. The reasons people give little (or nothing) to the church or to other charities are numerous and complex, but low-level giving is not simply a matter of who has money and who doesn't. Low-level giving exists in the most affluent zip codes nationwide.

(We'd like to recognize those who struggle financially, but who volunteer time at the church as a substitute. We're also going to exclude those who live in borderline poverty, though they often give anyway.)

We encourage clergy, lay leaders, and people in the pews to discuss the issue of disproportionate giving in your church. Can such an imbalance possibly be a life-sustaining state of affairs? We think not, and believe this discussion is long overdue.

Be forewarned, however, that members in the lower two-thirds of the donor ranks are unlikely to participate in such discussions. Church leaders should also not expect rational discourse to miraculously alter long-standing giving patterns in the congregation as a whole. Change of this magnitude takes time.

But there needs to be a starting point. Avoiding the issue of disproportionate giving will further entrench the current giving culture, and ensure the amount your church raises today may remain similar in the months and perhaps years to come. Surprisingly, many people in the pews may be unaware that such a problem even exists.

Charitable giving is one of the great, unexplained mysteries of congregational life. Countless church members report that when funds are needed to fix the roof, repair the organ, or send the youth group on a mission trip, the money shows up. But church members are often resistant to increasing their annual support for the general operation of the church.

Human nature being what it is, people usually don't want to pay more for something they are getting for less.

Three reasons why people give little, or nothing

First, low-level giving is persistent because the amount a person or family gives today is often determined by the amount that person or family first pledged to the church, perhaps many years ago. This is giving out of habit, instead of a spiritual discipline.

As noted, one of the primary breakdowns in American Protestantism occurs when people join the church. Membership committees are often reluctant to recommend an amount that new members should give. The message is typically, "Just pledge whatever is best for you."

It's surprising how many churchgoers claim they have no idea what to give. This is a vital reason why churches should introduce tithing at the earliest opportunity. New members are more open to innovative ideas within the first 6-8 weeks than any other time.

If the church fails in this task, that new member or family, not knowing any better, might pledge $500. If they increase their giving by 10 percent each year, it will take almost a decade for these parishioners to reach the $1,000 mark. A doubling of their pledge still results in a contribution of less than $20 per week.

This $1,000 amount is not selected randomly. In many congregations, the median gift (the midpoint — half above, half below) is approximately $1,000. This means that half the congregation gives $20 per week or less. It's a stretch of the imagination to believe that 50 percent middle class congregants find giving $20 per week to be a financial hardship.

Some people claim that parishioners give little to the church because they give so much elsewhere. We have not found this to be the case. A $250 donor to the church is unlikely to be a $5,000 donor to the United Way.

In their landmark study on giving to churches, titled *Passing the Plate: Why American Christians Don't Give Away More Money*, sociologists Christian Smith and Michael Emerson cite that one in five self-identified Christians gives nothing to the church, charity, or other non-profit organization.[2] It makes us wonder what their definition of Christian actually is.

The data also show that most American Christians, regardless of wealth, do not believe they have the resources to tithe. This brings to mind the quote by John D. Rockefeller, who said, "I couldn't have tithed the first million had I not tithed the first one-hundred." And, of course, there's the ironic comment made by a flabbergasted parishioner when the subject of tithing came up, "I make too much money to tithe!"

Returning to our $500 donors, the family in question might have their kids baptized in the church. Those kids are provided childcare on Sunday mornings, and may attend Sunday school and perhaps sing in a children's choir. In the meantime, a family member may have met with the minister for a personal matter. All this for ten bucks a week. It's like the cable bill, only it never goes up. Despite all the church provides, family members may remain unconvinced to increase their annual support.

Over time, this family's income and assets may have increased, but low-level giving has become an established norm. Many donors renew the same amount they gave the previous year, without considering whether this is an adequate sum or not.

During the 20th Century, giving as a percent of income did not keep pace with inflation. While real wages quadrupled during the 1900s, giving to church as a percent of income actually went down.[3]

Those who increase their pledges usually do so at a lower percentage than those who decrease. The most frequent pledges are $300, $600, and $1,200. These are $25, $50, and $100 per month, respectively. We suspect these gifts are routine, a matter of habit and not of the heart. Is it truly unreasonable to ask a $25 monthly donor to give $50 monthly? Or a $50 donor to give $100? Or a $1,000 donor to give $2,000?

> Many congregants give small amounts for years on end. We urge parishioners, at all gift levels, to double or even triple their annual pledges.

Financial planners claim that middle class Americans could double their charitable giving to all causes, and not notice the slightest difference in their daily lives. If your church doubled its annual pledge drive, you could fund a walk-in health clinic in a marginal neighborhood that would improve the lives of thousands of people. This type of mission is within your congregation's reach, or in partnership with churches in your neighborhood or region. More money actually does mean the possibility for more mission.

Returning to what church members should give, some denominations publish giving guidelines. These guidelines include charts with income levels and giving percentages, ranging from low to high. However, many of these charts list four categories of membership, from a "standard" level to the "leadership" level. Also, some charts begin at one percent of income. If you give people permission to be vaguely committed and give very little, they'll take you up on the offer. Don't provide this choice.

Back to the basics

All this gets us back to expectations of membership. If church members, new and old alike, are asked for little and don't understand their roles, people will go off in myriad directions and congregational life becomes a matter of herding cats.

Such a scenario can lead to factions within the congregation, some of which might be quite vocal about their consumerism. They want what they want (more interesting sermons, different music, better coffee, fewer harangues for money) and are unhappy when they don't get it.

Lacking a higher calling, a church can become inward looking, with a principal focus on maintaining harmony within the ranks. It's not uncommon for church members to say this is the pastor's key role.

We do not intend to be overly critical of the church. Rather, the scenarios we present are institutionalized bad habits that have remarkable staying power. The issue at hand is whether church leaders will confront detrimental norms that have developed over time, or leave them in the dustbin of history.

The subject at hand

Let's delve a little further into the bottom two-thirds of congrega-tional donors. Congregational minister Stephen Gray observed that half of congregants are relatively inert. They rarely show up, and have little to do with the ongoing life of the church. With rare exceptions, the uncommitted souls contribute the least, often making token gifts at best.

Yet experienced ministers know full well, often painfully, that inac-tive members (an oxymoron, and a membership category that should not exist) can be the most demanding. These are the ultimate consumers. They expect the full range of services the church has to offer, including pastoral attention, and the church being available for weddings, memorial services, and other special occasions. They some-times believe the church is a platform to lead programs on their pet projects, often unrelated to the mission of the congregation as a whole. Hand massage, anyone?

Of course, all this comes at a low cost or no cost because they're members. Aren't churches lucky to have them?

Such people take far more from the church than they give in return, and are perfectly content doing so. Why not? If someone else pays the freight and does the heavy lifting, what more could a church consumer desire? In contrast, we wish to dispel the myth that high-level donors expect special favors from the minister and the church because they give more. People who give the most rarely ask anything in return.

Seasoned ministers also realize that the most gripes originate in the lower donor ranks. This is one argument why clergy need access to the pledge figures, to consider the source. Another is determining who might be good leaders. The last person a church should have in a lead-ership role is a low-level donor from a high-income household. That person will be first in line to say that new ministries cannot be started because there's little money, and that church members cannot be asked to be more generous.

It is remarkable how frequently a few church members speak for the financial circumstances of all other members, with little knowledge of anyone's means, or their inclination to give. Clergy who do not have access to the pledge figures do so at their peril.

It may be disheartening for clergy and lay leaders to look around on Sunday morning and realize that half the parishioners in sight take more from the church than they give in return. This is one important reason against publishing the average pledge. That dollar amount is skewed disproportionately by a handful of large pledges at the top, and by excluding non-donors at the bottom.

Social psychologist Robert Cialdini writes that reporting the average creates an unspoken "magnetic middle" that has a tendency to draw people who deviate from the middle to it.[4] For example, the average pledge conveys the message that everyone in the pews contributes about the same amount. Nothing could be further from the truth. And by the way, when did God call us to be average?

Many church people realize their giving is admittedly ordinary, but may rationalize low-level giving by thinking that as long as someone else makes up the difference, the budget is eventually passed, and congregational life goes on as before, what difference does it make?

Church members who give above the average may adjust upwards only marginally, usually because they don't want to get too far ahead of everyone else. Calculating and publishing the average pledge is an exceedingly poor church policy; far better to educate people about generosity as a spiritual discipline.

The fallacy of meeting people's needs

We've already addressed the subject of low membership expectations as the fundamental reason why people give very little. Added to the list are churches that inadvertently play into the consumer mentality. To their detriment, churches convey the message, "We hope you like us. We hope you like the minister's sermons, the music, and the Sunday School." If not, the church must have fallen short. It didn't meet your needs.

Attempting to meet peoples' needs is one of Protestantism's great shortcomings. Churches are not in the personal satisfaction business. Perhaps a reminder is in order: the purpose of a church is not merely to serve its members, but rather, to call its members to serve, to cata-pult them from the routine of their daily lives into a state of being they cannot experience anywhere else. Church people are not birds with broken wings, and should not be viewed as such. Nor should they be catered to.

A photograph of a beautiful church in England expresses this sentiment magnificently. Carved into the stone above the front door is the phrase, "Servant's Entrance." This is truly God's word for us.

Old-line Protestant faith traditions have a long and ennobling history. But too often, the church has lowered its standards in an attempt to be all things to all people. In doing so, the church is depriving members of the selves they seek, of their very souls. This is a profoundly consequential religious matter, both for individual parishioners and for the future of Protestantism as a whole.

> *Church leaders create a congregation in their own image, for better or worse. To create an authentic church, clergy and lay leaders should call their members to lives of dedication, commitment, and when necessary, sacrifice for the greater good. For this to happen, clergy and lay leaders themselves need to set an example.*

Protestantism desperately needs to reclaim its rightful heritage of breaking the bonds of ignorance and prejudice, taking firm stands against injustice, and creating a church that is an unmistakable force for good in the world. None of this will happen if the church is a comfortable, convenient, inexpensive (or free!) stopover for middle class members, many of whom are the most privileged people this planet has ever known. Was the life of Jesus about comfort and convenience? We think not.

It breaks our hearts when we hear church people who are safely ensconced in the middle class say, "We should take care of ourselves first before helping anyone else." As though they are the ultimate consumers of all the church has to offer, with no responsibility to others outside their circle of fellow congregants.

A realistic timeframe

Preaching a gospel that challenges prevailing member attitudes might be a controversial route, though it really needn't be. Some members may get angry and leave the church. (Perhaps not a great loss.) As previously mentioned, others might question the authority of the church to delve into such matters.

But we urge courage and fortitude, for much is to be gained. Also, the changes we advocate are not going to take place overnight, so a vigorous dose of persistence is required. Clergy and lay leaders who wish to embark on the journey of creating more equitable giving should assume a three-to-five year timeframe. Change will be gradual, but the tide will turn. However, recognize that:

> *More equitable giving will not come about unless the membership committee is staffed by stalwart souls who convey to newcomers how their lives have been changed forever by the church, and promote Membership in Good Standing. The membership committee is not just an ordinary assignment. It is a high calling and a special ministry.*

Communities of faith hold the rightful authority to set standards that guide our behavior as religious people. This includes the belief that merely being a consumer, whether in church or in our daily lives, is antithetical to people of faith.

The second reason people give little or nothing is because they have no interest in the subject whatsoever. It's like they're wearing suits of armor. Nothing the church (or anyone else) can say or do will make the slightest dent. Recognize it when you see it, though keep a watchful eye if these parsimonious members expect and yea, demand, special favors from the minister and the congregation. Churches should be accepting of all souls, but are not doormats for those who audaciously take advantage of the congregation's good will.

The third reason people give little or nothing is because they are fearful. We'll address this subject in the next two chapters.

CHAPTER 3

The Good Life

There's a basic paradox of economic growth: as people do better,
they are often less content, because they expect more.
— *New Yorker* magazine financial columnist James Surowiecki

Robert Wilson, an investor *par excellence,* said the most boring thing to do with money was just spend it. He planned on giving away his entire $800 million fortune.His viewpoint is not exactly a majority opinion. For millions of people, shopping is the All-American sport; salvation at the swipe of a plastic card.

We're not going to berate readers for having what used to be called "nice things." Nor will we advocate that churchgoers wear sackcloth and ashes and lead a life of deprivation. However, we do ask readers, especially parents of children and youth, to thoughtfully consider the attitude that frequent trips to the mall constitute the good life — no matter how alluring the toys. Indeed, for what will it profit a man if he gains the whole world yet forfeits his soul? (Matthew 16:36)

Two ways to approach the good life

The first way is, "How much stuff do you need?" This is an interesting question, but with limited utility. In America, the size of cars, pickup trucks, houses, furniture, garages, meals, soft drinks, television sets, storage units, shopping malls, movie theaters, 24/7 cable shopping channels, sports stadiums, parking lots, and rates of obesity among children and adults alike have grown larger each year. Thus, countless souls may answer the question of how much they need, with, "I'll shop 'till I drop."

Financial guru Dave Ramsey urges fiscal restraint to his six million radio listeners, and paints those who overspend and incur unneeded debt as, "Weak-willed, self-indulgent, and stupid."[1] We'll let Ramsey have the last word on this one.

The second issue is more fruitful, deserves greater consideration, and includes a number of life-altering questions posed by the imaginative Lutheran educator Bob Sitze. He frames it in theological terms by posing the following questions:

- How's it going, really?

- How do you decide what's important in life, and what isn't?

- How much longer can you keep living the way you're living?

- What's broken in your life and not getting fixed?

- What would it take for you to try something new, really new; or something important, really important?

- Are you ready for the power of honest, emotional conversation as the central element by which all important change happens?[2]

These questions enable people of faith to focus on a central theme in the book's introduction: What kind of people God is calling us to become? What do we want God's opinion of us to be, and how do we wish to be recognized in the estimation of our children, family members, friends, neighbors, and colleagues?

Sitze believes that churches of all faiths can be places whose central identity might be described as: we help you live a just, manageable, and sustainable life. He uses the word sustainable not in an environmental context, but rather in the context of individuals and families creating loving, healthy, long-lasting relationships in God's eyes.

We believe this is the work of the church. Such an emphasis in congregations could become a central purpose that binds members more closely together in community. (It should go without saying that the greater the tendency toward individualism, the weaker the community.) Moreover, this description of the church compliments and energizes traditional theological formulations of the church's essence that focus on worship, preaching, and the sacraments.

Are we ready for this kind of conversation?

Questions like those on the previous page are rarely included in a church's religious education program for adults. We believe they should be.

This is because a critical element in making the annual pledge drive obsolete is shifting away from asking church members for money, and inviting them to commit to a different and more fulfilling way of life. A dominant subject of this book is that it's not a matter of the church needing money, but the yearning of people to develop an authentic relationship with God.   *Community ?*

So what's the eventual goal?

We know people of significant means who are quite happy, and some who are miserably unhappy. We also know people of lesser means who fit these categories, as well. So happiness and leading a fulfilling life do not depend on how much money you have in the bank.

Like knowing good art when you see it, we experience generous people and families from all socio-economic backgrounds as having an engaging fullness about them, somewhat difficult to define, but very perceptible. Generous people have a sense of peace about themselves. Forever giving, they are attentive to others, thoughtful and kind, lack prejudice, are slow to criticize and quick to forgive, and seek the best in the people they encounter. They always seem to have time for others, and often volunteer when help is needed. Even if you're middle-aged, you hope that when you grow up, you'll be like them.

Generous people could buy more expensive houses, cars, or clothes, but usually don't. They tend not to worry about anyone breaking into their house and stealing anything, because other than photo albums, heirlooms, and keepsakes, nothing is all that valuable. If they do splurge, it's usually on world travel.

Noted psychologist Karl Menninger once commented that over many decades working in mental health, he didn't ever recall having a generous person as a patient.

We're not psychologists and certainly can't claim that being generous will result in better mental health. But it's a sure bet that the obsession for a satiated life, a manicured life, or a life of excess will eventually prove barren. Fifty years from now, few will remember how much money you had, what kind of house you lived in, or what kind of car you drove. But the world might be a better place if you were important in the life of a child, or a lost soul.

Countless surveys, including longitudinal surveys of the same people over many decades, reveal one consistent measurement of happiness. That measure is warm, caring relationships. Financial success and material goods rank considerably lower on the list of factors that create individual and family contentment.

In his book, *A Whole New Mind,* author Daniel Pink writes:

> For most of human history, our lives were defined by scarcity. Today, the defining feature of social, economic and cultural life is abundance. Abundance has brought beautiful things to our lives, but that bevy of material goods has not necessarily made us happier. The paradox of prosperity is that while living standards have risen steadily, decade after decade, personal, family, and life satisfaction haven't budged. That's why more people — liberated by prosperity but not fulfilled by it— are resolving the paradox by searching for meaning.[3]

In our view, the good life should be about an innate sense of simplicity, caring, and love for one another. Is this really so difficult for churches to foster?

Robert Wuthnow is Director of the Center for the Study of American Religion at Princeton University. His words will resonate with those who desire the church to speak with more clarity and conviction on this topic. He writes,

> Clergy lament the materialism of our society and the pressures to work harder and spend more. They worry that young people are being corrupted by false and misleading values of the marketplace. They acknowledge that wealth and generosity do not go hand in hand. Most clergy realize there is theological support for these opinions. Still, they find it hard to say anything that might criticize the ways their parishioners are living.[4]

Noted theologian and author Parker Palmer echoes this theme, believing that acquiring ever more can have ruinous consequences. He writes, "We cling jealously to our share, even if it is more than we will ever use. Arrogance tells us that we need even more. The result is a corrosive consumerism, a drug of choice, all the while discovering that material goods will not bring meaning to our lives."[5]

A difficult struggle

Battling the culture of American consumerism is a Herculean task. Each year, Americans see and hear some 38,000 ads for consumer products. This is heady competition for the once-a-year stewardship sermon.

Advertising to grown-ups is only a segment of the industry. Parents are now encouraged to buy electronic devices for 3-year olds. Fourth-grade girls are dieting, and 10-year olds believe that if they don't have Facebook pages, they're nobodies. If this isn't corrosive consumerism, we don't know what is.

In a recent editorial, *Harper's Magazine* editor Thomas Franks remarked that back in the 1960s, during the heady days of Madison Avenue ad campaigns, "There was a notion that prosperity itself was hazardous to our health. But now, these worries seem kind of quaint — the stuff of vaguely remembered sermons about materialism."[6] Maybe it's time to revisit those old sermons.

Making the annual pledge drive obsolete will be an appealing option for many clergy, lay leaders, and people in the pews. Church leaders often wonder (sometimes out loud!) why people don't just do what they know they're supposed to do, and support the church without repetitive appeals. But doing away with a long-entrenched church custom can be exasperating, even if a better idea comes along.

The following points are designed to prompt conversations that clergy, lay leaders, and people in the pews could profitably have with one another. If preached only from the pulpit, these seeds will likely fall on rocky soil. Sorely needed are respected souls from the pews who can model, recommend, and advocate the rewards, joys, and yes, even the sacrifices sometimes required for a religiously committed life.

What do you mean by a different life?

The church should encourage its members to achieve debt-free living, the ultimate freedom that allows us to pursue lives of greater meaning and purpose.

The following conversation starters are designed for people of all faiths, apart from politics. Admittedly, they do challenge the notion that Americans will have infinite resources, everything they desire for as long as they live.

• Many churches offer programs on how to create and sustain happy and healthy marriages; how to raise children in an electronic age; how to create and maintain positive family relationships; how to handle your money; how to understand the latest healthcare laws; how to recover from divorce; and how to grieve when a loved one dies. All these bring God into the daily lives of all His children, so we can help one another down life's pathway.

• Churches can offer classes in alternative ways of living. The Voluntary Simplicity movement strives to make simple lives more socially acceptable, unencumbered by soul stifling "stuff" and onerous debt. Living simply has gone beyond the stereotype of wearing Birkenstocks and eating lentils and tofu. For example, the newly coined word, "frugalista" refers to people who delight in the challenge of living exceedingly good lives on very little money.

• Whatever your means, is it absolutely necessary to purchase the biggest and/or most grandiose houses, cars, furniture, clothes, technology, and other consumer goods you can afford?

• We hope churchgoers will reclaim Sunday as an old-fashioned Sabbath. Once home from church, we urge individuals and families to refrain from commercial activities such as going to the grocery store or the mall, and if possible, not to drive your car for the rest of the day. The Sabbath is a great blessing for busy, overworked families.

• To literally save a life, we encourage churchgoers of all faiths to donate blood on a regular basis. Will your congregation challenge other churches in the region, to see who donates the most?

• A well-documented fact is that reducing consumption of meat, and taking up a partial vegetarian diet results in better health. Plus, approximately seven pounds of the world's resources are required to produce one pound of meat. This is a matter of good health, and stewardship of the earth on which we live.

• Church members may wish to consider "zero-scape" (*xeri-scaping*) landscapes for their homes. This landscaping requires considerably less water and few, if any, chemical fertilizers or pesticides, and is an extremely attractive alternative to traditional green lawns.

• We urge church members to engage in mission projects; locally, nationally, or abroad. Sometimes it takes participating in an out-of-town or international mission to open our eyes to seeing local mission opportunities.

• Will church members view ostentatious displays of wealth and consumption as antithetical to the religious life, and not succumb to advertisements that equate having ever more with achieving the American dream?

• We encourage parents to teach these values to their children. We also urge parents and grandparents to help younger generations learn to become generous, giving souls.

Numerous surveys indicate that churchgoers and non-churchgoers alike *lead almost identical lives.* If we live our lives no differently than our un-churched friends and neighbors, what difference does the church make? What's the point?

People who lead lives that confront the prevailing consumer culture will be the vanguard of a forward-looking church, and a major force for good in American society. These hearty souls will help restore the church's legitimate voice at a time when Americans desperately need an alternative point of view.

Will clergy, lay leaders, and church members themselves take up these challenges? The issue is not just the amount one gives to the church. The issue is using all the resources at our command to craft lives of meaning and purpose. Thus, it's not just the five or ten percent we give to the church, but what we do with the remaining 90 to 95 percent, as well. Stewardship is an all-year calling to a new way of life.

Mainline churchgoers rank among the most well educated, successful people who have ever walked the face of God's green earth. What better legacy can we leave our children and grandchildren; than to be generous people who took great pride in creating a bighearted church that welcomed all who entered, and served the world in ever greater measure?

Finally, about 150 people at a regional meeting were asked if they would make a sacrifice for a larger cause or a greater good. About 95 percent of people answered, "Yes, I would." Many added, "I wish my church asked this of me." We rest our case for increased giving and a distinctive, religious way of life.

CHAPTER 4

Why Some People Give
and Some People Don't

Charity is enjoined upon each of us, not just the rich,
or those who can be said to afford it.
Charity can be learned at any time in life.
— UCC minister Joan Clark

A friend of ours, one of four children, grew up in a rural town that had a sizable population of people who were recognizably poor. Her parents, non-churchgoers, often gave their children extra food or money to share with kids at school. Years later, as grownups, all four are comfortable financially. Two attend church, tithe, and have great empathy for those less fortunate. The other two wouldn't give a starving man a dime. Their attitude is that people who get themselves into trouble should find their own way out.

We wonder how these children turned out so differently, but suspect that many readers observe a similar dynamic in their own families, regardless of means.

A fundamental assertion of this book is that churches should be places where people are made whole. As for where we become inspired to give, church is a good bet. Ronald Lundeen, a Presbyterian minister and church consultant, makes the observation,

> *My experience in religious and secular organizations is that,*
> *regardless of faith tradition, people in religious communities are*
> *more inclined toward generosity than those who are not. Religious*
> *faith is a common denominator among exceptionally generous*

people. In my experience, those most adept at articulating their religious experience are correspondingly generous.

Lunden's comment is strikingly similar to that of Episcopal priest Andrew Cooley. Upon taking up a new parish, he was pleased to observe congregants coming to church with an "adult faith." Pinpointing a person's faith development to becoming a generous person isn't an exact science, but we imagine there's a strong correlation.

In one of our own surveys, we asked people why they are motivated to give to the church. Their responses are quite instructive:

"My relationship with God, and knowing the church makes a huge difference in the world."

"How happy my church makes me."

"Doing the right thing is what God calls me to do"

"Realizing the blessings that God has given me."

"Serving God's people."

"My love for God, and the freedom I have to practice my faith."

"God himself. He gave it to me, and I give it back."

"I learned to give as a child, and it has been a way of life as long as I can remember. I thank my parents every day."

If your congregation hasn't provided the opportunity for such testimonials, we urge you to consider this practice.

As for churchgoers who remain miserly, it's our contention they are unable to articulate their religious faith adequately. The reasons are difficult to determine, especially if they've been coming to church for a considerable length of time.

Some harsh realities

Numerous observers of philanthropy in America believe the main reason people give little or nothing is fear — fear of not having enough money, whether tomorrow, next week, next month, next year, or later in life. Many Americans, for a host of reasons, live with financial anxiety every day.

For a sizable group, the most reprehensible cause remains the Wall Street debacle of October, 2008. Millions of people saw trillions of dollars disappear from their pensions, home values, and savings. As of this writing, some have recovered, while many have not.

Without glossing over financial hardships that people face, we might wish to keep them in perspective. In particular, we wonder if middle class churchgoers unknowingly manufacture attitudes of fear and scarcity that negatively affect their day-to-day lives, and limit their spiritual growth, as well.

Lynne Twist, in her excellent book, *The Soul of Money*, relates the Three Toxic Myths of Scarcity. The first myth is based on the false assumption that there's not enough to go around. The existence of big box stores alone should allay this fallacy, but the prevailing consumer culture dictates that there's not enough: not enough time, not enough money, not enough clean air or water, oil, landfill space; not enough (fill in the blank).

If there's not enough, this leads to the Second Myth of Scarcity: More is better. I'll get mine before someone else does. We perceive fewer things in the midst of plenty. This competition finds its ultimate horror in a store clerk being crushed to death by a horde of shoppers, and fist fights in the aisles of retail stores.

The third Toxic Myth of Scarcity locks the other two in place: that's just the way it is. We are not responsible for our actions. We have no control over accumulation. It is a natural law—survival of the fiscally fittest.[1]

The Great American Dream

Let's return to the American advertising industry, and its increasingly provocative ads and commercials. If you purchase the right products, you'll have perfect hair, skin, teeth, houses, cars, lawns, vacations, spouses, and children. You'll be deliriously happy every waking moment and even while sleeping because of the perfect sleep medication or ultra-fabulous mattress, knowing you are vastly superior to the unfortunate souls who made inferior product choices.

The incessant drumbeat of these ads portrays well-to-do families as the norm. If you don't live in an idyllic Norman Rockwell town, life has passed you by. These ads create two additional fears among the citizenry.

First is the fear of never achieving the Great American Dream and *NO* living a life of inadequacy, for not having an idealized lifestyle that exists only in a fantasy world presented by the media. In 1854, in *Walden*, Henry David Thoreau wrote, "The mass of men lead lives of quiet desperation." We suspect this is still true today.

If you find yourself in this category, our prayer is that you achieve peace of mind by not comparing yourself with others who own more material possessions, but on the essential and durable assets of love and caring for those in your midst, fed by and founded on a day by day, ever-growing relationship with God.

The second fear, particularly among those who have put their noses to the grindstone, labored relentlessly, and made great sacrifices to achieve an exceptionally high standard of living, is the fear of losing it all. *NO*

Over the past few decades, by adding more and more hours to their weekly schedules, Americans now work a full month longer per year than in times past. Today, sixty-hour workweeks are commonplace.

The Pew Research Center states that 68 percent of middle-class Americans list "more free time" their number one priority. Yet only 14 percent of American workers took vacations of two weeks or more, and 57 percent took only one week or more. TimeDay.org states:

> *Men who don't take regular vacations are 32 percent more likely to die of heart attacks, and 21 percent more likely to die early of all causes.*

> *Women who work long hours also have a heightened risk of heart attack.*

> *Stress and burnout are five times more costly to treat than average workplace maladies. (www.timeday.org/right2vacation/care.asp)*

Busyness is now the American badge of honor. (A related issue but not one relevant to this book is the family-unfriendly work environments

guilty?

in most parishes, with clergy working excessively long hours, sometimes seven days a week). Beyond health issues, the upshot of overwork is significant. Spouses, children and other family members are short-changed by parents and other grown-ups who are absent from the home for long stretches of time.

This reminds us of the boss who, upon hearing complaints from employees about crushing workloads, noted, "There's always time after midnight."

After working all these hours and accumulating all these costly possessions, a heightened fear is added to the mix — protecting what has been gained. This fear has given rise to gated communities, sophisticated alarm systems, increasing numbers of security cameras, private security police, and heightened paranoia of anyone who doesn't look like they belong in the neighborhood.

Who gives what, and to whom?

Ken Stern is an attorney, author, and nonprofit executive. His recent book, *With Charity for All: Why Charities Are Failing and a Better Way to Give,* highlights a number of issues that are pertinent to our conversation. For example:

> In 2011, the wealthiest Americans, those with earnings in the top 20 percent, contributed 1.3 percent of their incomes to charity.

> Those at the base of the pyramid, the bottom 20 percent, contributed 3.2 percent of their incomes to charity.

Stern writes, "The relative generosity of lower-income Americans is accentuated by the fact that, unlike middle-class and wealthy donors, most of them do not claim the charitable tax deduction because they do not itemize deductions on their income tax returns."[2]

But there's a deeper interpretation behind these figures, one that has a silver lining. Stern finds that the wealthy may be less generous because the drive to accumulate wealth is inconsistent with communal support. In 2011, not one of the top 50 individual charitable gifts went to social service organizations, or to charities that served the poor and dispossessed. Instead, these gifts went to prestigious colleges and universities, medical centers, arts organizations, and museums that cater to the nation's and the world's elite.

Stern also finds the isolation of wealthy donors, especially those who live in homogenously affluent neighborhoods, is a factor in being less generous. Here's where the silver lining comes into play. When low and high-income donors watched a sympathy-eliciting video on child poverty, the compassion of the wealthier group began to rise, and both groups' willingness to help others became almost identical.

Might this be a head's up to clergy and lay leaders whose churches are in the most affluent communities in America? Might we become inspired to be more generous if we better understood the plight of those we pass on the street everyday? It would be a blessing to communicate stories of successful outreach ministries to parishioners on a regular basis.

Should people be fearful or not?

We'll end this chapter with a few more facts and figures, then give our bottom-line answer as to whether middle-class churchgoers should worry about giving money away or hanging onto it.

According to a USA Today article of March 23, 2013:

- A greater number of Americans are living debt-free, but those in debt owe about 40 percent more than in 2000

- In 2012, the American savings rate was 3.9 percent

- For 55 percent of Americans, savings outweigh debt

- For 24 percent of Americans, debt outweighs savings

- Sixteen percent of Americans have neither debt nor savings

- Median family debt nationwide is approximately $70,000

- Among 35-44 year olds, the median family debt is $108,000

- About 43 percent of American households spend more than they earn

- The average American has 3.5 credit cards

- Average credit card debt is $15,950

- About 40 percent of Americans carry credit card debt from month to month

The most consistent finding was that approximately 25 percent of households in all income levels, from the richest to the poorest, have more debt than savings. How many Americans, as the saying goes, are two paychecks away from losing it all?

And the answer is . . .

Regarding whether people should be fearful of giving away money, here's our view. If the 2008 financial crisis was devastating to you and your family and you're still recovering; if you've lost your job or are working for a lower salary than before; if you were retired and returned to work because the value of your pension declined; if you're barely keeping your head above water; or if financial obligations keep you awake at night; then you might consider taking a pass on charitable giving until things get better.

In the meantime, you might seek credit counseling to help alleviate your financial anxiety, and perhaps start a program at the church to help others who are in a similar situation, *to help them rise above their own fears.* Isn't this what churches should do at their core — help people address their fears?

Most people struggle financially at some time during their lives. Nevertheless, the human heart has an inherent need to give. We know of a woman in Arizona who cleaned houses for a paltry $750 a month to support her family, and who tithed $75 a month to her church. When the pastor suggested she stop doing that, she replied, "Don't tell me I cannot give to God." For people of all means, charitable giving can be extraordinarily healing to the heart and soul.

On the other hand, over the past five years, if you've:

- Bought a more expensive home, or a second home

- Renovated your current home

- Bought a new car or boat

- Sent your kids to expensive private schools
- Have season tickets to a professional sports team, symphony, or ballet
- Enhanced your wardrobe with upscale clothes and jewelry
- Own multiple computers, smart phones, and wide-screen TV's
- Belong to a private gym
- Have traveled abroad

You can probably reach the 5-10 percent charitable giving level without compromising your standard of living. As one Episcopal bishop noted, regarding "snow bird" residents in his warm-weather diocese who came down from the north, "If you can afford two houses, you can afford two pledges."

The next chapter suggests a few places where you can invest some of that money that might be lying around.

CHAPTER 5

How Churches Can Become Worthy Recipients of Parishioners' Charitable Giving

People respond to grace more than anything else.
— Presbyterian minister Wayne Rhodes

If churches wish to become worthy recipients of members' charitable giving, what must they do? This can be a surprisingly thorny question. It makes perfect sense that schools educate students, or that a manufacturer makes widgets. These are clear and unmistakable goals. A church's call to ministry, however, is considerably more difficult to define.

That's because each church is a distinctive, idiosyncratic community of souls, with a unique geographic location, personality, history (for better or worse) and quirks. There's not a one-size-fits-all answer to how a church becomes a credible, trustworthy, deserving recipient of members' charitable support.

We're uncertain whether mainline churches understand what is required to retain the trust, loyalty, and commitment of members. Over the past 50 years, mainline denominations have lost millions of adherents, and the church's influence in contemporary society has diminished precipitously. We needn't dwell on the many reasons. Most readers are well aware of never-ending clergy scandals, along with ministers whose extremist views paint all religions with a broad brush, making the un-churched wary of considering any church of any faith.

[handwritten margin notes: "In Midwest a bubble of ... soc/econ"]

Unfortunately, the problems that beset traditional churches don't stop here. Church observer Randell Boone notes, "The reasons people stay in mainline churches and keep them propped up are more often sociological than religious. Sociological factors have to do with family history, business friendships, preferences in music and architecture, a desire to associate with those who have achieved a similar level of education, and in general, the tendency to maintain the outward signs of one's social class."

Novelist Kent Haruf writes of the small church in particular. In his book, *Benediction,* he makes the observation, "People don't want to be disturbed. They want assurance. They don't come to church on Sunday morning to think about new ideas or even the old important ones. They want to hear what they've been told before, with only some small variation on what they've been hearing all their lives, and then they want to go home and eat pot roast and say it was a good service and feel satisfied."[1]

David Roozen, a prominent sociologist of religion, adds yet another perspective, especially in regard to theologically liberal churches. He notes, "I don't think liberal theologians and church leaders have made the case for why religion adds anything to a liberal lifestyle. Why do you need the church to volunteer at Habitat for Humanity? Why do you need the church to tell you that gays are equal to any other person?"[2]

We don't mean to pile on, but it's important to acknowledge the epic problems facing mainline churches today. John Buchanan, editor of *Christian Century*, wrote, "Christians owe one another more than basic civility, because we operate under the mandate to love one another with enough visible authenticity that the world will be attracted to the faith we profess. What the world sees of the ways Christians disagree (mainly on gay rights) is far from impressive, and sometimes repulsive. It must make Jesus weep."[3]

A fundamental reason why churches have diminished in stature is their inability to define their role and purpose in this place and time. For example, countless church boards and committees gather together each year to write or renew their mission statements. Some denominations have lengthy guidelines that require the better part of a year for a committee to complete its work.

[handwritten margin notes: "Why we E should give"]

Despite these guidelines, committee members eventually discover their mission statement is similar to other churches in their denomination, and surprisingly comparable to other churches in town, even of different denominations. It's as if some invisible force keeps church leaders and people in the pews from looking into their hearts and souls, to determine their unique calling, role, and purpose.

Can you recite your church's mission or vision statement? In most churches, these statements remain vague, little known, and virtually meaningless because they have never been actively considered or internalized.

If your church fits any of the above descriptions, some soul searching is in order, because if people don't believe in the cause, they won't buy in. St. Paul puts it, "If the trumpet gives an uncertain sound, who shall prepare himself for battle?" (1 Corinthians 14:8)

Our favorite mission statement is, *Every Member a Ministry*. This means that each and every person in the pews has a role to play.

Some interesting alternatives

Instead of cursing the darkness, let's light one small candle, and that candle is your church. We'll consider a number of ways in which your congregation, of any size or faith tradition, can inspire greater trust and generosity among its members. We'll begin with whether or not people in your pews feel empowered to begin new ministries.

Some years ago, author and social commentator John Gardner wrote widely about American society. His views are prescient in regard to the church, as well. He wrote, "Society is not like a machine that is created at some point in time and then maintained with a minimum of effort. A society is being continuously re-created, for good or ill, by its members. This will strike some as a burdensome responsibility, but will summon others to greatness."[4]

Does your church summon people to greatness? Or have church members accepted a tranquil uniformity as the norm, or feel limited because money is always in short supply, or frustrated because hidebound committees squelch new ideas, or stymied because vocal minorities oppose every new idea, or because clergy lack confidence in their calling?

This book is not a comprehensive assessment of congregational life. However, it's important to note that bad habits of long standing definitely exist, and persist. Each of them dampens a congregation's spirit and lessens members' enthusiasm for supporting the church financially.

Let's look at some of these bad habits, and consider three alternatives.

Trust?

I. Saving one soul at a time

Countless first-time church visitors say they were completely ignored by parishioners around them. Being unnoticed in a crowd seems to affect single adults in particular, who claim they feel lonelier in church than anywhere else. Isn't that a sad statement? If people, single or otherwise, visit your church and experience loneliness or indifference once, they're unlikely to return for a repeat performance.

Most churches claim they are friendly. More precisely, current members are friendly to one another but standoffish to outsiders. Most churchgoers don't come to church on Sunday morning thinking they will introduce themselves to strangers, and some may not be keen on this idea at all.

However, creating a welcoming culture in your church is eminently attainable, and should be a high priority. Every person in the pews, even the most introverted, can be that one compassionate soul whom God has called upon to rescue another who is lost and lonely.

We encourage your congregation to create a culture in which reaching out to the stranger becomes second nature. Church shoppers have many choices. Don't let that one chance with a visitor pass you by.

> *Maybe the essence of church should be saving one person at a time, one wandering soul who discovers the presence of God in his or her life.*

Theologian Samuel Wells writes of this very issue.

> *"By committing themselves to meet regularly together, Christians become aware of those who are not gathering together — those*

our
challenge

who are absent. This is how a community develops the practice of pastoral care and evangelism, the skill of memory for those who are missing, the virtue of love for the lost, and the notion of the communion of the saints."[5]

Many obstacles in this path

Your church may not be aware of those who are missing, or the virtue of love for the lost. If so, this means your congregation falls below its God-given potential to bring others into the faith. There are few good reasons for neglecting The Great Commission. The typical reasons churches cite for not being recognizable beacons of hope in their communities are all too mundane. A few we hear often include:

"Nobody around here has any interest in evangelism."

"We've never done outreach like that before."

"We're a happy family and like the church the way it is."

The unspoken attitude about the un-churched is usually, "If people are lucky, they'll find us. If not, there's nothing we can do about that, is there?"

This prevalent view often produces membership plateaus and a long-term sameness in congregational life, because there's little new blood. Actually, the reasons for a lack of interest in outsiders aren't reasons at all, but excuses, and not even particularly good ones. A plethora of excuses diminishes God's presence in a congregation, and may cause members to drift away because the church does not stir their hearts or souls in any definable way.

Will those who remain support the church with only the minimum required to maintain the institution? Many churches are kept afloat by one-third of members who give sizable amounts, often the more elderly members. Such churches too often live by the tyranny of the operating budget, all those things they cannot do because there's little money. Such a life can be dispiriting and soul deadening. Surely, this is not what God is calling the church to be.

II. Lives of meaning and purpose

Mother Teresa once said that loneliness and not being valued are among the most debilitating aspect of anyone's life. Today, we suspect people are lonely in their real lives, and even more so in the ubiquitous world of their electronic devices.

Alienation is a common theme in both fiction and nonfiction. In a short story by Joyce Carol Oates, the main character doesn't even have a name, and is known only as, "The man." She writes, "The man had been director of a laboratory for many years. His work was predominant in his life. He was famously generous to younger students, a legendary mentor to his graduate students. He'd never been married. He wasn't sure he'd ever been in love. Though he'd always wanted children, he had none. He was dissatisfied with his life outside the lab. He felt cheated and foolish, worried that others might pity him."[6]

Theologian Parker Palmer writes that after a decade of war and political divisiveness, he began to feel like a displaced person in his own country. He bemoans the American tendency to distrust people from beyond our borders, and viewing others as aliens. He summarizes his feelings by saying, "Perhaps we all share an abiding grief over some of modernity's worst features: its mindless relativism, corrosive cynicism, disdain for tradition and human dignity, and indifference to suffering and death."[7]

Palmer continues by saying that many people, himself included, "Are afraid that our inner light will be extinguished or our inner darkness exposed, and we hide our true identities from one another. We lead divided lives, separated from our souls."

In doing so, he says, "We sense that something is missing, and we feel fraudulent because we are not in the world as we truly wish. Too often, we turn to anesthetics of choice — substance abuse, overwork, consumerism, and mindless media noise."

Is there anything the church can or should do about this?

Most of us have felt as Palmer does. Where is one to turn with such feelings? To church? We certainly hope so, but are required to ask what mainline churches have to offer as a remedy.

The acclaimed Old Testament scholar Walter Bruggeman speaks of this very issue. In a recent lecture he said that people come to church with feelings of loneliness, despair, uncertainty, and unresolved anger. They attempt to face life's challenges with honesty and integrity, but feel inadequate to the task. They are dismayed at seeing greed and evil in the world triumph. They believe their feelings need to be acknowledged, to be honored.

What they too often find is a church that offers up timid prayers and anemic meditations. They hear, "Be still before the mystery of life" on Sunday morning. They listen to the soothing words of walking beside still waters rather than, "My God, my God, why hast thou forsaken me?" Bruggeman believes that, "Pain needs to be brought to light in order for people to be made truly whole, to experience the depth and meaning of the religious life."

So the question is, if people struggle with their spiritual lives and are feeling estranged from society, should they not find clarity, resolution, and redemption in the church? If not, where else will they turn? To the mall, to television, to drugs, to the Internet, to professional sports, to working ever longer hours? Surely, these are wretched substitutes.

Through its programs, small group ministries, classes, retreats, worship, and service, the church must take a considerably more activist role in helping congregants, both young and old, newcomers and old-timers alike, find God. How, indeed, do people determine what is important and what is not? As simple as this question appears, the answer requires a community of people who take church seriously, people who will not settle for a lukewarm faith.

"One way to establish community is to enable people to live a rule of life," notes author and Episcopal priest Jerry Doherty. He continues,

> Having a rule of life enables people to see themselves as being able to pray, grow, and work in ways that make a difference because they are one with God. It is living a rule that shows the importance of living in community. [The rule] contains the measure by which the people conduct the practice of their religion and also by which they evaluate how well they are doing.[8]

Fundamental Fairness

Such work is not just for clergy, church boards, or committee chairs. This important work is also that of rank and file members who feel empowered to begin new ministries because they have a longing or an ache in their hearts and know others do, as well.

New or exciting initiatives are an excellent way to stimulate giving in any congregation. This is often easier to accomplish in larger churches with more resources. But smaller congregations can also launch new efforts. Most often, a sense of urgency toward a desired goal is an excellent starting point. If an initiative is truly important, church people will find a way.

For example, many small congregations have discovered a partic- SCA ular "vocation," such as adopting a school, creating a simple plan to welcome those who are new to the community, or forming a supportive Active relationship with an organization that supports the homeless. Some have planted community gardens and started soup kitchens. Others employ a part-time parish nurse.

We know of a congregation that adopted its first responders, and prepares an annual "thank you" meal for them. Another rural congregation offers a weekly spaghetti supper that is open to all, and as a result has seen its Sunday attendance grow, as well as its influence in the community. Such vocations can be a motivation for creating a generous congregation, one that will consider "second mile" giving, an attractive antidote to established, same-level giving.

For these reasons, we urge congregations to begin a New Opportunities Seed Fund, to provide working capital for people in the pews to assume leadership roles in creating and sustaining the larger ministry of the congregation. This fund should be well publicized, so all will know the church encourages their participation in the work of the church.

Any church of any faith that is viewed as lifesaving and life transforming will never worry about money. If a church perceives its call to ministry in a straightforward and authoritative manner, the money will be there.

III. The church should give more to the outside world

In the introduction, we mentioned that the healthiest and happiest churches give a larger than average share to mission and outreach beyond their own four walls. How do some churches achieve this, while others fail? As mentioned, one of the worst things that can happen to a congregation is to become inwardly focused, with church members being concerned only about themselves.

Let's provide two examples. The first is a church of 165 members in a suburban town with a median household income of $49,000 and a median family income of $67,000. The church's budget is $325,000, quite large for a congregation of that size. The line item for outreach in the budget totals $42,000, about 13 percent. Beyond the budget, members give an additional $65,000 to support two schools in Central America, and members make frequent trips there, paying their own expenses. This is an astonishing record of service for a congregation of this size.

When we spoke with the minister, she said she didn't talk about money all that often. Her ministry was focused on people finding a genuine relationship with God. If that occurs, ministry to the outside world becomes a given, in that being a generous person or family is a natural offshoot. Every time we visit this church, highly visible posters, banners, photos, and displays about their mission efforts are in plentiful array. It is at the core of who they are as people of faith. Church members give repeatedly to multiple ministries throughout the year.

In contrast, we know of a 400-member, multi-generational church that is hearty and healthy, with excellent music, a strong family orientation, and an annual budget of $565,000. The median household income in this town is $95,000 and the median family income is $118,000. The church's annual operating budget contains no line item for outreach or mission beyond its own four walls.

In years past, on random Sundays, church kids who were Girl Scouts or Boy Scouts might show up in their uniforms after the service, selling cookies or popcorn. Or the youth group would set up a car wash to raise money for a local homeless shelter. Or high school students would do odd jobs to raise money for a mission trip. Most church members enjoyed having these energetic kids around, and were happy to spend a few dollars now and then for a good cause.

However, a number of church members complained they were always getting hit up for money. The church board discussed the matter and voted 5-4 to discontinue all youth-related fundraising initiatives at the church. Was this a good decision or not?

These two very different churches illustrate an extremely important principle: generosity begets generosity, and conversely a miserly attitude is surprisingly efficient at reproducing itself. All too often, clergy and lay leaders act as the protector of members' pocketbooks. Instead, their job should be to create a church that serves the world in ever-greater ways, and models this desired behavior to its membership. This is the church's true mission.

A final, stunning example is the Memorial Drive Presbyterian Church in Houston, Texas. Their policy is to give one dollar to the needs of the world for every dollar it spends to benefit current members. This is not a five percent line item for outreach, nor a ten percent line item. This is a 100 percent line item. Most churches nationwide could follow this example. Might you be the one to introduce the idea in your church?

Three practical ways to expand mission

The church's leadership should approve the following at the earliest opportunity.

First, congregations should give away the plate offering each Sunday (excluding gifts designated by envelopes and checks for pledge payments) to mission and outreach in the local community. In doing so, parishioners will be successful in their outreach efforts every time they gather in community.

Churches that give away the cash offering often experience four and five-fold increases in the collection plate, and an increase in the annual pledge drive. Committing the Sunday offering to outreach will not rob Peter to pay Paul. This is a powerful ministry, and people in the pews will take great pride in what they have accomplished together.

Second, congregations should also assign at least 10 percent of their operating budgets to mission. This should be the first line item in the budget, and the first to be paid. All other line items follow. Outreach should not come last, if there's anything left over at the end of the fiscal year. Do not let a single person say, "We can't afford it." If that belief prevails, your church will become evermore inward focused, and will have a limited future.

This practice models what we ask Members in Good Standing to do. If the institution of the church is unwilling to commit 10 percent, what message does that convey?

To help accomplish these two goals, we urge church leaders to drop the term "operating budget" and replace it with, "Financial Statement of Mission." This is not just semantics. The term operating budget suggests a business model. The goal of a business is to make a profit; the goal of a church is to transform lives. These divergent goals require significantly different perspectives.

To adopt the phrase, "Financial Statement of Mission" changes the entire way churchgoers view and spend money, and puts into words that seemingly mundane line items such as "overhead" are, in fact, essential investments in the mission of our church. We cannot transform lives without facilities, staff, programs, and especially our worship and outreach expenditures—but it's all mission.

Third, calculate and publicize the amount of money given to outreach per member. This figure is one of the most telltale indicators of your congregation's call to service. It's simple math to add up the amount of money given to outreach from the offering plate, plus the amount given through the line item Financial Statement of Mission. Divide that sum by the number of current members.

Be forewarned that the per-member figure may be very low. However, calculating this figure may be a blessing in disguise, a signal call that God believes your church can do considerably better. This figure can be a motivating factor in the church taking on new and more substantial ministries, which in turn will raise the level of charitable giving overall.

A word to the wise: clergy and lay leaders should never use low giving figures to scold a congregation, as in, "These numbers are terrible and you should be ashamed of yourselves." However, if a few highly regarded congregants hint that the congregation could be better perceived in the eyes of God, this would be a very good thing. In fact, a prompt to those highly regarded parishioners might just be a clever move on the part of church leadership.

On a closing note, we urge our Christian readers to consider the Jewish tradition of *tzedakah*, which translated from the Hebrew means "righteous deed," or "righteous giving." Traditional Hebrew faiths view charitable giving as a matter of duty, an expectation that involves honor and justice. Whether this is your theology or not, as heirs of a Judeo-Christian tradition, we acknowledge that such a perspective encourages us to keep God in our hearts and souls each and every day. And won't we be the better for it?

CHAPTER 6

Practical Ways of Ending the Annual Pledge Drive

If you always give, you will always have.
— Chinese Proverb

Let's begin by determining who's currently responsible for raising money in your congregation. If your church relies on the conventional pledge drive, whether in the fall or spring, it's logical to assume the Stewardship Committee is charged with the task. They're the ones who publish brochures and pamphlets, prepare charts and pledge cards, make announcements on Sunday mornings, ask for money, send acknowledgement letters, and oversee the process from beginning to end.

In kicking off the pledge drive, the committee hopes the minister will deliver a highly inspirational stewardship sermon. Since committee members wrote a better stewardship letter and came up with a more persuasive theme than last year, hopes run high that parishioners will increase their giving.

Sometimes these hopes are fulfilled but more often they're not, for a couple of reasons. First, many congregants don't show up for the stewardship sermon because they claim they've heard this message before, too many times. Even if congregants are in church, a good sermon, alas, usually doesn't result in increased giving, except among those who are already the most generous.

Second and more importantly, the pledge drives rests on one bedrock issue:

Success in the stewardship realm is ultimately the responsibility of the minister(s), board members, and lay leaders of the congregation to define the journey upon which the congregation is embarked.

The Stewardship Committee is only the vehicle that conveys the leadership's message of hope for the future. If that message is strong, your church is likely to be successful in any endeavor, financial or otherwise.

If that message is weak or ambiguous, the stewardship committee is adrift. Committee members are on their own to conjure up one theme or another, and themes can be wildly inconsistent from year to year. A theme-of-the-year pledge drive also signals that the congregation views life one fiscal year at a time, rather than as a community of faith on a journey characterized by a distinctive way of living over many years.

The appeal to the congregation for financial support, more often than not, will also be an appeal to support the operating budget. This is a terrible idea, unless you've substituted Financial Statement of Mission for operating budget.

Even then, the budget itself, in all probability, is the end product of numerous compromises, a watered-down document based on what things cost rather than mission. Church budgets rarely envision anything that is markedly different from the previous year, and mainly focus on institutional maintenance.

In addition, every line item in the budget can be a disincentive for giving because penurious parishioners, often at the annual meeting, have been known to inquire, "Why do we have to spend so much money on X or Y?" Sometimes these comments are nickel and dime in nature, about snow removal or air conditioning; but sometimes they are directed toward the pastor's compensation package, which can throw a congregation into turmoil as this raises the question of the pastor's competence.

. The upshot of the low-cost budget is the congregation's hopes and dreams go unfulfilled. God's hopes and dreams for your congregation also go unfulfilled. This can create a congregation that more or less goes through the motions, focusing on routine transactions that are similar to those of years past. We're not saying an accurate budget is unimportant. Rather, those line items, paying the church's bills, are not a motivation for generous giving among people who are charitably inclined.

One example we'll cite here with admiration is the Assemblies of God. Members are asked to give directly to God, and what the church does with the money is largely irrelevant. There's a leap of faith, one that is not limited to a particular faith tradition. We've discovered this attitude frequently among the most generous donors to churches of many denominations.

In contrast to the once-a-year appeal, well-informed church leaders should present a continual array of new and captivating ministries that energize a congregation. In churches like this, charitable giving is a year 'round process that helps congregants engage with people not yet met, and the wider world.

Secular nonprofit organizations operate from this vantage point. When you receive mailings from a local hospital, your alma mater, or an agency that serves those who are less fortunate, there's always something new afoot. These mailings convey captivating stories and provide donors with innovative and exciting opportunities to give. Churches would do well to emulate these methods.

> *If your congregation's primary focus is on current members and there's little urgency about anything in particular for eleven months of the year, it will be well nigh impossible to mount an inspiring pledge drive in the twelfth month, no matter what the theme or the stewardship sermon.*

The time, effort, emotional energy, and angst invested in the annual pledge drive are exceedingly poor investments of the church's resources. How such a scheme, one that is remarkably good at creating low-level donors has remained in place for decades is truly bewildering.

Alternatives to the annual pledge drive

The fundamental flaw with the annual pledge drive is that it's a "one size fits all" approach. Rich or poor, employed or unemployed, stable or unsteady, hopeful or in despair, the pledge drive's message supposedly falls like rain upon each soul equally.

An apt analogy is a financial advisor who utilizes only one investment approach for all clients, of whatever means. Churches, like investment advisors, need to offer an array of choices because a person or a family's finances, like stewardship, is multi-faceted and people approach it from myriad perspectives.

Below are a number of alternatives that, taken in one combination or another, will assist your congregation in moving away from the repetitive, one-size-fits-all pledge drive. Please be reminded that the following are not just different ways to ask people for money.

Charitable giving emanates from the heart and soul, and a way of live worth living. It is not simply a matter of the pocketbook.

Let's look at each recommendation in turn. We urge readers not to reject any single idea outright. Similar to ice cream flavors, you may not like strawberry vanilla, but someone does, otherwise it wouldn't be on the menu. If you're in a decision-making role, please don't deny a fellow church member a charitable giving option because it's not one that you favor personally.

In fact, parishioners may find themselves choosing more than one option, and wouldn't that be wonderful? The recommendations presented are not mutually exclusive. If you choose one, the others don't disappear.

It's important to note that any combination of the choices below won't end the pledge drive overnight. Congregations will need to continue some form of the annual drive until church members adjust to alternate ways.

Allow members to pledge anytime of year.

Church members are grown-ups and can spend money whenever, wherever, and however they wish. They don't need to wait for the annual pledge drive to roll around. Members can make, renew, or increase their pledges anytime. What could be simpler?

As for increasing pledges or making extra gifts throughout the year, who says that can't be done? Why should church members be limited to pledging only once a year? Congregants who are deeply moved by something eventful at church can express their appreciation at any time — winter, spring, summer, or fall.

This simple, clear-cut method places great trust in members of the parish, and encourages them to do the right thing. Such an approach will be attractive to those who currently pledge the most, because pledge drives too often contain repetitious, sometimes annoying, and occasionally dire appeals from the pulpit and in the newsletter. These appeals are usually directed toward people who haven't turned in their pledge cards, typically recalcitrant parishioners in the middle to low donor ranks.

Such appeals are ineffective because they are akin to attentive students in a classroom listening to the teacher scold miscrants in the back row. Churches should not play this losing game, because the noncompliant souls in question are probably not in church and don't read the newsletter, either.

We tested the giving-any-time-of-year recommendation via a survey to dozens of churchgoers, and the idea holds interest and potential merit. Some, however, claim it would be difficult to formulate the operating budget without a clear idea of how much money is coming in. Our hope is that church leaders will take this small gamble, because parishioners are unlikely to reduce their current level of giving only because the pledge drive has been changed around.

Other survey respondents believe that human beings are natural-born procrastinators, and need structure around their charitable giving decisions. This may be true. We hope congregants will rise to the occasion on their own initiative. Occasional reminders in the newsletter and from the pulpit are certainly acceptable.

One option is that most software programs offer a calendar feature that can be set up with "tickler" reminders, to nudge people about the timing of their pledges. This enables members to review, contemplate, and pray about their financial commitment without having to turn in their pledges on one designated day, or within a short period of time.

Some congregations may wish to retain the power of an "ingathering" or pledge dedication Sunday, which builds enthusiasm for the cause. Such occasions may be scheduled every three or four months, as part of the routine of community worship life. The purpose of these services is not to seek financial support alone, but also to highlight the church's many mission programs because of the generosity of members.

These ongoing services are an excellent way to model to newcomers and current members alike that any time of year is an appropriate time to reconsider the gifts that God blesses us with, and what we do with them.

Finally, on this particular subject, some respondents believe the annual pledge drive is an excellent vehicle through which to communicate the church's hopes, dreams, and needs for the future. They are correct. However, communication of the church's role and purpose is essential throughout the year, no matter what method of stewardship is employed.

Members can give as they receive.

This is one of the most promising and engaging means of charitable giving ever devised, and should be widely discussed in your congregation. Using this approach, when people are paid, whether weekly, twice a month, monthly, on commission, on contract, with a bonus, royalties, year-end compensation, interest or dividend income, or in any other form, they write a check for a percentage of what they have just received.

The payoff of this option is immediate gratification. Instead of making a routine pledge payment or utilizing an electronic funds transfer, like paying a utility bill, people get to make a brand new charitable decision every time they get paid!

For example, during one pay period, a person or family's funds might be in short supply due to unexpected expenses, so the percentage given may be less. Over the few next pay periods that family might be flush, and the percentage could be considerably higher. Each payday,

family members get the privilege of making a decision about how charitable giving ranks as one of the cornerstones of their religious lives.

Being generous should imply giving, "happy money." Happy
money is what you spend on a gift for a loved one, or for a special occasion. This contrasts with sad money, often associated with having to
pay a parking ticket or getting rid of termites in your house. Church
families should support the congregation with happy money. It's much
more fun.

Speaking from experience, the practice of giving as you receive can
create evocative conversations among family members. These conversations are a constant reminder that all we have comes from God.
Parents who involve children in charitable decisions discover this is an
excellent way to incorporate generosity as a family value. It's also an
extremely effective way for younger generations to inherit positive attitudes toward money from their elders. Who wants to raise stingy,
materialistic kids?

This reminds us of the book, *The Power of Half: One Family's
Decision to Stop Taking and Start Giving,* by Kevin and Hannah Salwen.
Prodded by 14-year old Hannah's incessant exhortations about
inequality in the world, her exasperated mother finally said, "What do
you want us to do, sell the house?" To which Hannah replied, "Yes."

The family sold their 6,500 square foot landmark house and moved
into a nondescript house of less than half the size. In doing so, they
committed half of the proceeds, $800,000, to a dozen villages in
Ghana, one of the poorest regions in the world. A year later, Kevin
Salwen described his powerful emotions upon seeing his daughter and
a 70-year old tribal chieftain cut the ribbon to a new corn mill in that
African country.[1] "And a little child shall lead them." (Isaiah 11:6)

The Salwen's contention is that most middle class American families
could give away half their assets and still live comfortable lives. Might you
be the brave soul who introduces this idea in your congregation?

Over-the-transom money.

Some congregations receive checks in the mail out of the blue, for
amounts ranging from $100 to tens of thousands of dollars. Hand-

written notes that read, "I came into some extra money, and would like the church to apply this amount to an area of greatest need," frequently accompany these unexpected gifts.

Such gifts are extraordinary gestures of love and compassion. Churches receiving unexpected gifts tend to be those with trusted leadership, that currently give a larger than average share to mission and outreach. This would be an interesting subject to introduce in your congregation. How might your church increase its odds in receiving over-the-transom gifts?

As the holiday season approaches, members should be encouraged to contribute to the church's outreach programs (not the operating budget) the same amount of money they spend on holiday gifts for their friends, colleagues, and family members.Of course, this is above and beyond one's current giving, an add-on.

One of the most abhorrent aspects of contemporary American culture is Black Friday, the day after Thanksgiving, the most important day on the retail calendar. Black Friday, and the days leading up to Christmas, is marked by a relentless barrage of advertisements that urge frenzied Americans to pack the malls at midnight and scorch their credit cards for holiday gifts. Cyber Monday is now on the rise, as well, when on-line retailers offer specials on the Monday following Thanksgiving. Giving Tuesday, an antidote to shopping, is gaining in prominence, but occupies a far-distant third place.

By giving away one dollar for each dollar spent, individuals and families can balance every dollar in proportion to the others. If spending for consumer goods subsumes charitable giving, we become lesser people in the eyes of God; our hearts and souls shrink a bit (maybe a lot); and our capacity to accomplish good in the world diminishes.

In decades past, people were urged to save 10 percent of their incomes, give 10 percent to the church, and live on the remaining 80 percent. Financial planners still urge this as a sound money practice. Returning to this elemental formula might become a goal of congregants in your church.

Members should reach the 5-10 percent giving level as soon as they are able

This relates to Membership with Integrity, applies to current members, and to new members coming in. Don't let anyone tell you that no one in the congregation can possibly afford it.

Encourage members to include the church in their estate plans

To grow an endowment or a rainy day fund, church leaders need to make some important decisions regarding the use of money derived from estate gifts. The first is whether an estate gift will automatically be placed into a permanent endowment, or if portions or the entire amount of the principal can be spent.

People frequently leave money to a church or nonprofit organization and do not specify how that money should be used. This can be a mixed blessing. An unexpected gift can throw a church into a quandary if gift policies have not been previously established. We're aware of too many congregations that became engaged in bitter disputes over the use of an unanticipated bequest. Sadly, a generous gift becomes a source of strife, a dreadful state of affairs.

The second question is whether interest income from an estate gift, if placed into a permanent endowment, will provide annual, unrestricted support to the church. Or will this money be used only to start new ministries, or provide a matching incentive for large-ticket capital projects? Some churches urge members to endow their annual unrestricted pledges, while others believe current members should pay their own way.

Churches that set up independent foundations to receive charitable gifts rarely allow interest income to be used for operating costs of the church. There are no hard and fast rules. Your congregation will need to make some judgment calls here.

Speaking of no hard and fast rules, we're familiar with a 3,000-member Methodist church in a wealthy community whose bylaws prohibit the formation of an endowment fund. They believe the church is not a bank, and that God's work is in the here and now. On the other side of the spectrum is the Consortium of Endowed Episcopal Parishes, an organization that encourages churches to begin and manage endowment funds, some of which involve hundreds of millions of dollars.

We'll add a note that some readers may consider surprising. Churches can have too much money. Many of the most deeply troubled congregations are the wealthiest. Be careful what you wish for.

On that note, the late Rev. Peter Gomes, minister of Memorial Church on the Harvard University campus, oftentimes announced the Sunday offering by saying to his well-heeled parishioners, "Some of you out there have more money than you deserve, so here's the chance to put some of it to good use."

The charitable giving culture in your congregation has evolved, for better or worse, over many decades. Old-timers and newcomers alike may give lesser amounts because no one asked them to do otherwise. So it's no one's particular fault that low-level giving is the norm. It is our contention, however, that when people of faith are challenged in a positive manner, they will respond. For example, "We need to leave this particular legacy behind, and work together to better accomplish God's will for us."

We'd like to close this chapter and the book with a few words from United Methodist minister Paul Nixon, who wrote about churches having, "The passionate conviction that we offer something that will renew human lives and communities; and the belief that God sent us to this particular place and moment for a reason."[2] If this is the defining context of your congregation, money will be a secondary concern. It will be there when needed. Guaranteed.

References

Chapter One

1. Miroslav Volf, "Way of Life," *The Christian Century,* November 20 - December 3, 2002. 35.

2. George Barna, *Evangelism That Works: How to Reach Changing Generations With the Unchanging Gospel.* (Ventura, CA: Regal Books, 1995), 51-52.

Chapter Two

1. George Barna, *The Second Coming of the Church* (Nashville, TN: Thomas Nelson Publishers, 1998), 19-20.

2. Christian Smith and Michael Emerson, *Passing the Plate: Why American Christians Don't Give Away Much Money* (New York, NY: Oxford University Press, 2008)

3. Smith and Emerson, *Passing the Plate, 42*

4. Robert Cialdini, Noah Goldstein and Steve J. Martin, *Fifty Scientifically Proven Ways to be Persuasive* (New York, NY: Simon and Schuster, 2008) 26-29

Chapter Three

1. Dave Ramsey, "Personal Finance: How to Manage Household Debt," in *The Week Magazine*, November 15, 2013, p. 35

2. Bob Sitze, *Starting Simple: Conversations About the Way We Live,* (Herndon, VA: The Alban Institute, 2007), 22-24.

3. Daniel Pink, *A Whole New Mind: Why Right-Brainers Will Control the Future* (New York, NY: Penguin Books, 2006)

4. Robert Wuthnow, *The Crisis in the Churches: Spiritual Malaise, Fiscal Woe* (New York, NY: Oxford University Press, 1999), 230.

5. Parker Palmer, *Healing the Heart of Democracy: The Courage to Create a Politics Worthy of the Human Spirit* (San Francisco, CA: Jossey Bass Publishers, 2011)

6. Thomas Franks, "Easy Chair," in *Harper's Magazine*, August 2013, 5.

Chapter Four

1. Lynne Twist and Teresa Barker, *The Soul of Money: Reclaiming the Wealth of Our Inner Resources* (New York, NY: W.W. Norton, 2003)

2. Ken Stern, "Why the Rich Don't Give," in *The Atlantic*, April 2013, 75.

Chapter Five

1. Kent Haruf, *Benediction* (New York, NY: Alfred A. Knopf, 2013), 193.

2. David Roozen, "Century Notes," in *The Christian Century*, August 3, 2013, 15.

3. John M. Buchanan, "Editor's Desk," in *The Christian Century*, November 13, 2013, 3.

4. John M. Gardner, *Self Renewal: The Individual and the Innovative Society* (New York, NY; W.W. Norton Publishers, 1995)

5. Samuel Wells, "Improvisation: The Drama of Christian Ethics" from his blog titled, Samuel Wells @ Faith Matters.

6. Joyce Carol Oates, "The Mastiff," *The New Yorker*, July 1, 2013, 60.

7. Parker Palmer, *Healing the Heart of Democracy,* 76.

8. Rev. Jerry C. Doherty, *A Celtic Model of Ministry* (Collegeville, MN: The Liturgical Press, 2003), 64.

Chapter Six

1. Kevin and Hanna Salwen, *The Power of Half: One Family's Decision to Stop Taking and Start Giving* (Boston, MA: Houghton Mifflin Harcourt, 2010)

2. Paul Nixon, *I Refuse to Lead a Dying Church* (Cleveland, OH: The Pilgrim Press, 2006), 17-19.